I0760024

In a Riptide

In a Riptide

Ronna Bloom

Brick Books

Library and Archives Canada Cataloguing in Publication

Title: In a riptide / Ronna Bloom.
Names: Bloom, Ronna, 1961- author
Identifiers: Canadiana (print) 20250213907 | Canadiana (ebook) 20250213915 | ISBN 9781771316583 (softcover) | ISBN 9781771316606 (PDF) | ISBN 9781771316590 (EPUB)
Subjects: LCGFT: Poetry.
Classification: LCC PS8553.L665 I52 2025 | DDC C811/.54—dc23

We gratefully acknowledge the Canada Council for the Arts, the Government of Canada through the Canada Book Fund, the Ontario Arts Council, and the Government of Ontario for their support of our publishing program.

Edited by Sue Sinclair.
Author photo by Cylla von Tiedemann.
The book is set in Fournier.
Design by Marijke Friesen.
Cover art by Hawu Lim in collaboration with Sua Kim: 도시인 080 | City Dweller 080, 2021, Digital drawing on screenshot of Instagram post.

Brick Books
487 King St. W.
Kingston, ON
K7L 2X7
www.brickbooks.ca

Though much of the work of Brick Books takes place on the ancestral lands of the Anishinaabeg, Haudenosaunee, Huron-Wendat, and Mississaugas of the Credit peoples, our editors, authors, and readers from many backgrounds are situated from coast to coast to coast in Canada on the traditional and unceded territories of over six hundred nations who have cared for Turtle Island from time immemorial. While living and working on these lands, we are committed to hearing and returning the rightful imaginative space to the poetries, songs, and stories that have been untold, under-told, wrongly told, and suppressed through colonization.

Table of Contents

The Earth Held Me: *dead person*

Don't Close the Door to the Door to the Door: *happy person with nothing*

Immeasurable

Today a woman of no measurable age stopped me
to ask where she could buy some meat, and her eyes
filled up with tears when it seemed too far or impossible
and every shop was closed. I could do nothing but stand there,
vibrating in the hesitant spring. We were just two more
meandering women in the empty street. Some of us
looking down as though illness could pass through the eyes,
others looking up, sending out our million help-me messages.
We stood there with nothing obvious passing between us
but time. Then she smiled and went away.
And I thought of the four people the Buddha met in his travels:
sick person, old person, dead person, happy person with nothing.
And I felt like all of them.

To Show the Scars:
sick person

An Excruciating Blue Day

All April, the one purple pansy clung on
in the hail. It waved its silky elements.

A spider with elegant legs appeared on my ceiling.
There you are again, I said. *Or is this your daughter?*

I don't speak spider, but tried to coax one from the sink
then gave up and flooded it. Yes, there's an edge to my voice.

It's too cold for the spring I want. My mother asks
when she can see me again, demands a date.

Just for today, I will be the World Health Organization
and have all the answers.

For anger, take a hit of helium. For bitterness, mimic
the dog's lolling tongue, then watch his reaction.

When you find a tumour, ask the barista at Second Cup,
Is there a cancer discount for that?

For sleep, lie down if possible.
For sadness, dance.

I explain: keep staring at the blue sky like it's your pain,
eventually it will change colour.

Vulnerable to

Shock

Call me gut-sharked and simped out. I can't
sleep. I'm a death bucket of news,
lolograssing in my sheets.

Her tumour in my earphones yesterday
stopped my leg paddles on the path.

Night and coherence don't mix.
What is health? Make a drink. A frick
of toast with peanut butter.

Anyone can be a dictionary of myths.
There's a hollow earth in this open grapefruit. Pink
with juice and ligature. Acid in the gorge.

I resist poetic redemption. Let it be this.

Wonder

An x-rayed tumour on a spine
looks like a wad of gum on a radial tire.
Will it be cut out like jam from hair?
The doctors are called Savage,

Pain, Wonder, and Shepherd.
Where will they take her? Will they leave her alone?
There is a causeway, a footbridge.
I stay on my side.
She sleeps and might wake.
She slips and may fall.
She as she was, was.
I hug her but do not break her.
She is your sister too.

Area 3

A man is called to Area 3.
He walks in after his wife, slowly
pushing his walker.
His running shoes squeak on the floor
and his black sweatpants are loose.
Because I know what kind of doctor this is
I know what part of the body is being touched.
I feel like both the wife and the husband.
I march ahead, then drag my feet. Afterwards,
outside the hospital on the long road
that runs north to trees, south to water,
I turn to look at myself
and wait for one of us to speak.

Therapy

Deprivation makes you fussy, the therapist said.
At the restaurant, the waiter asks,
Is anything ok here?

In my case I lie on the parapet of desire afraid to move,
for getting and losing are two sides of a coin.
You can't resolve a complex, Jung said, *you just outgrow it.*

Rilke sat up with me at night by the side of the road
and I felt better. He told me indirectly it would be
temporary. Then pointed to the house that once existed,

and which I could still see
because memory is like that. The house I grew up in,
turning into light like the cars behind us.

Afterwards I watched thousands of red-winged blackbirds fly east,
a black-red river in the sky.
When two flocks met, they swirled into a cyclone of birds
without reason or reply.

Lyrical Hospital

Who is your mercy contact?

Things He Said the Last Time We Visited

You smell like cloves and eucalyptus.
Please spray some of that in my sleeves.
I'll have a popsicle, lemon.
Do you have more of that foot energy?
Is the canister full?
Thank you.
I love you.
I like that sweater.
It makes sense you're here during these gnostic rituals.
I hope to go to Bridgepoint and have a big
end of life celebration with all my friends.
Do you consider yourself a therapist or a witch?
I've always liked citrus.
It's the earth's magnetic field.
You're like the mother I need now. You are
the mother I need now.
I'd like to try the mango lassi.

The Buddha Prepares for a Triple Bypass

Thanks the nurses for the antiseptic soap.
Whispers, smiling: *Don't worry.*
Have you seen my chest? Not a hair on it.
Nowhere for germs to hide.

Carries the bar to the shower, lathers. Hums to himself
a song. Not from the palace of his youth, nor the temples.
It's a sea shanty! The Buddha sings with gusto
and, after a scrub, emerges glistening as the waves.

Climbs back into bed, sees the attendant
with the furrowed brow and says, *It's ok, friend,*
there's room for suffering in love. And you know,
I didn't die of a broken heart. Let's go.

Holy Week

Tuesday I left my house and a whole lot of leaves from last fall
sped ahead like they were running to catch up with something.

Wednesday my sister had a Seder and read the plagues
without a hint of irony. I ate a frozen dinner at home.

Good Friday, it was reported that nurses
had the taste of death in their mouths.

Monks wore long brown robes and face masks
into the Church of the Holy Sepulchre.

On Saturday, a girl in the road was practicing
the names of days, changing their order
with her mouth power. *Tuesday is at the back!*

I lie awake with millions of other insomniacs,
marvelling that midnight belongs to no one.

Next week will also be holy.

Today in the street,

everyone looks like a Francis Bacon painting.
Their faces are occupied the way a country is.

The wind never really dies down.
It just moves to a place I'm not in.

My pen is not up to the task of sorrow.
My gratitude for the cup doesn't fill the cup.

The stunt woman with my name
hasn't gone nearly far enough.

Is It Safe?

Tell us, they said, no one died
or killed or took their life
and left it in the basement.
Tell us there are no people ghosts or creature ghosts.
Tell us what colour is a good colour and will we be safe.
Will a condo rise above? Or a sinkhole below?
Please tell us, they said, if you will leave the light on,
if you'll come back,
what you did here and with whom,
and will we be lovely, will we be lonely,
will we be lucky?
How much will it cost, they said, and how loud.
For how long, they cried, for how long?

In Crises

We put our heads down and try to work
our tiny magics.

Take our blessing pills, interrogate our crimes,
and commit new ones.

Between Fur and Skin

In the National Gallery, buffalo stood with their coats
thrown over their shoulders like ladies at a tea.
In another room camels. Came upon them unexpectedly
between paintings and ideas tied with string. Kept saying

camel, camel. Wounds
enlarged a thousand times to show the scars.
Art that plunged me into small dark rooms
with film scores and moving pictures.

But the animals were insistent. A goat smiled in a Chagall.
A million taxidermied birds posed or flew across the centuries.
And those standing buffalo, camels made of fake fur,
burlap, wire, and consciousness.

At a talk in another country, a woman begged the gathered,
Look out for those few creatures left.
Those with one horn, monstrous, wrinkled, fragile,
killed by the pound for the pound.

Another said, *Why*
should I give money to creatures I care nothing about?
And it was us talking from the bottom of our burnt-out souls
saying, *Who will care for us?*

The question hovered
and in the room burst out a shame, a pride, and baldness
pointing skyward, downward, straight ahead, behind,
in all directions, silently saying, *This is us, all this.*

The Blue Mark of Fever

The blue mark on the tiles is where
I fell in the bathroom holding the toothpaste.
The red bruise inside my lip is where
it hit the tub. The water is
from the broken glass on the way back to bed,
on the floor, in the seat of my pajamas.
I think it's from the glass but not sure.
The water is also from the fire in me.
The sigh is from my throat but no one hears.
I'm alone in the house. And it's night.
When the fever rose,.I fell. Everything let go.
At least I slept.
In the morning, when the sun came out
I cried for my friend.

Prayer

Out of this, let my small noun cry faith.
Let me unperson for a minute—
here, hold my cup.
Breathe me presence into the face
of my mother's tantrum of grief
that I can't answer any other way.
Her whine—let it be a song-plea
to the balladeers of other centuries.
O, how the cows moo in solace.
How the stars are greasing their sides
like skis getting ready for a long descent.
Send fire power for the fall!
And make me a right-now compassion rattle.
Hollow me out, Lord, for the sickness and the
sacred are the same path.

For Ten Billion Years:
old person

One Night

In one minute, I slept a whole night.
In one night, I slept a whole minute.

The world changed completely
while I was gone.

Dearly Ignored,

This message is being relayed to you from inside your cells
where you feel the ratcheting, the sour wounds.

Which of the many can raise their invisible mitochondria
and wave, *Me, I have been festering for ten billion years
since the dawn of the Pleistocene.* I believe you.

These are wounds recognizing wounds
saying, *We exist.*

Are we talking past lives? I have no answer.
But traces. Even without memory.

Once you were running in the desert and saw a hut
and thought it was near but you ran and ran and it was
still far. Near and far are so confusing.
Wounds are like that, constantly appearing on the horizon.

I can feel you wanting me to find something positive here.
Please, let's not rush.

Dearly Ignored, for how long have they misread
your name, calling you *Beloved* when you felt
none of it? This too is your birthright.
The wince of having been brought here and told, *Be happy.*

And the surprise when happiness indeed came
up within you like an infant singing in their bed,
their arms wound around their head.

But who can really remember being that baby?
Maybe in a dream, when you feel that lurch awake
in the middle of the night, you will know it's you
I've been talking to. Take in
a slow breath to know the air within you
is also around you. No better or worse. Same air,
ignored and beloved.

I used to know

how to talk to people. I used to feel
the underthing they were feeling,
and have the questions.
Now I don't know what to ask.

I live, like many friends, between urgency
and despondency. I sit with everyone
in the big asklessness, waiting
for birds to fly out of our mouths
full of velocity and direction—

for the reach of the mind
like an ocean that can't find the shore
or a shore that can't find the ocean,
lonely for each other,
in a riptide.

Speaking Vapour

I grew myself from vapour, borrowing skin
from every crone until I was grafted whole.
I knocked on lots of doors and one opened.
It had my body inside. I said, *You know what I am
and it scares you.* I was speaking vapour.

*I'm talking to you, body. I've treated you like a czar
would treat a peasant, and still, you carry me. I apologize.
I should live through a doorway under a low arch
where I bow my head every night to go in.
You've borne my shame with your sore back.*

Body said, *You know what I am and it scares you.
I am meat and flavour and decay. Others touch me.*
I bowed my head. Body took me to the hospital
for the sane, which committed me over and over
to poetry in its nakedness and expense.

Poetry is free but will cost you everything.
The body is free but will cost you everything plus itself.
And the body entered the soul and poetry entered
everything full of new affection.

Sisyphus Gives Up

Carry your own stone.

October in My 62nd Year

Anyone in this latitude knows the score:
October's bright burnt-orange trees and killer blue sky.
November's deadness. The SAD light comes next,
and a grease-flash of ice in the path.

What do I look forward to?
Metamucil in my gin and tonic,
a boiled egg in the morning, and a trail
of Werther's candies in a lap around the park.

In the mirror, I see: eyes, face, old woman,
the blown apart sky, Aunt Lillian
on a bench on Queen Mary Road, late in her life,
belonging so completely to herself.

The Past

Soon the year will be over, a rag thrown in the back
with the others. It'll be a number, shorthand for a quest
or a death. But now is summer, a day
in August. In the dreaming night

                                        I was in the exploded mouth of a city,
in a room forgotten, staking a claim to an anger
that tired me out.

I was in the park on the corner
drinking out of a paper cup, and I was meeting love
and touching its wrist.

I was speaking to a woman whose sister never came back.
I was asking a man what he fantasized, and he said, *I don't.*
I remember.
I was in a plane circling with nowhere to land, and on a tarmac
waiting.

I was in bed, where a man once lived, and when they rang the bell
he brought the carriage and the horse. Below me the ghost horse
I never knew.

                        The past is everyone's
ghost horse, and it keeps breathing as it carries us.

Dear Now,

Many people are trying to get in touch with you.
They have a lot on their minds. But you, dodgy fucker,
you keep coming up *no* or *ow*.
You, dazzler, shift and shift again.
Your function, if you have one,
is to mesmerize so we can't actually see you.

A flash of light strobes to my left as you
turn over beside me in bed, whisper *now*.
Did I see you? Did I turn around and turn
into salt? Could I stare into your eyes
like the eyes of the sun and keep seeing?

Something doesn't want me to look.
Over here! It motions to the last minute
or the next. Why so invested in invisibility?
Is this how you do your great and terrible work?
There's no tracking you.
You are nowhere and nowhere is now
here. I want to stay up with you all night
and get my questions answered.

The Future

One night in the last century, I dreamt
I sat on a high wall, an open book on the ground.
The sea rose. *Be careful of the book!* I called.
The water didn't care. In the dream, I had no boots.
To each her own footwear in the apocalypse.

Children are out mopping because there's no school
when there's no school. And the old, well, it doesn't matter
how tired and dazed we are, all we can do is all we can do.
The tide will turn. Fire and water and so on.

In Australia, fire burnt the paws of the koalas.
It ate the forests of Brazil, the houses of LA.
Thailand flooded. Italy too. In Venice, someone's couch
was swept into the water, someone's tombstone. Tourists
looted the Vuitton store and swam away with the goods.

Now is the time. Everybody swim.

Emotions at Work

Anger and exhaustion walk out together on the old road
in the rain.

Fear goes shopping, covers its mouth.

Grief takes a nap,
wakes up grieving.

Laughter is wandering the neighbourhood
where I live, and the one where you live,
trying to find some mouths.

Disgust is spitting on itself.
Don't look at me.

Love appears unexpectedly,
like the smell of pizza
when the box is opened

like a mountain after months of fog.

Service

The doctors are writing poetry.
The poets are listening to the stories of soldiers.
The soldiers are changing the sheets of the aged.
The aged are dying as trumpetlessly as ever.

And if you could rub their feet,
that may be all you could do, but it is a lot.
Their feet get very cold where they are going
and then get very still.

Quiver Fish

Some quiver fish in my belly begins to speak
in its own voice: don't ransack me or slur me
onto your dock for filleting or flaying. i'm a beginner.
i bubble to surface. vertical is the way up
and the way down and sideways.
i live a cross-hatched life.
you can see it in my gills and the rings
around my eyes. i'm old.
the turtle of fishes, but tiny.
i swim to understand. *onism* means
you can be only in one body. not true.
the whole school is in me and i am in the school.
copper glint, bronze shimmer. blue.
not only am i more than one, but also less.
flakes of me move downstream
into your veins and lake out.
you mistook this rippling for fear.
let me learn every tail-thrash of the way.

For the young man who looked into my face,

take it all.
Leave no remainder.

The Earth Held Me:
dead person

Five Elegies

After she died, the psychiatrists
gathered in a big room
and revealed their fallible humanity
to her sister, and listened

really listened to how red
her ecstasy
when no one was looking.
How riddled with red she could get.

And the psychiatrists maybe
envied her a little
even in their confusion and sorrow.

And the gentleness that had been missing—
for her, within her,
for them, within them—
was there.

~

He knew the gossip in the street, worried for the children,
loved his smokes, dug a bed for no flowers
but was one, sort of.

~

You took the passwords and mental strong boxes with you,
the money numbers and backstory. Your being
was the illusion of my safety.

Tiredness is not going away for any of us
back here on the ground. The world keeps spinning.
When I open my ears, the woe flows in.

I swear to God, there's a new bud
coming out of the orchid I had to cut down.
I can't be sure. It's pink inside.

~

They were dancing inside the pub six or seven of them
falling on each other lassoing each other's necks
stumbling kissing each other's heads. They were drunk so drunk
they couldn't stand but so drunk they could dance.
Like trees pulled up in a storm, swaying in water,
they looked dangerously unhappy, like they could drown.
They had been abandoned by sun and crops and government
and sobriety. The clocks ticked but no one stopped.
No one saw me watching from the window, the bitter rat poison
in my pocket, the rain pelting down, my future behind me.

~

When I heard you died,
I was sitting in a chair in the garden
with the phone to my ear. I got up
and lay on the grass, saw nothing, but earth
held me as it will you.

Nobody's Job

When you were dying, I held up the phone and a voice said,
We love you. We're proud of you. Go free.
And you scattered.

Moments before, you held up your hand
and I read our future in your palm.
Our paths wandered up your fingers and scattered.

The stars shushed each other.
The moon turned on her usher's light,
and the road went on.

*

When I was grieving, I saw
that it was no one's job to take care of me
however sad I got.

Surprised. I'd thought we all had someone
or that everyone's job was to look after everyone.
But it's not true.

And I gathered myself
and sent myself everywhere
and went free.

Rending the Garments

There should be a *shiva* for every kind of grief—
the break-up, the diagnosis, the assault—
where people come over unbidden and
wash their hands and bring casseroles
and hold you.

They do this all day or three times a day
for seven days so you know, you know
it happened and matters to more
than you, matters to a community of you.

What's needed is wailing with an axe, fights,
outings, and touch. Touch and singing.
Can you hear me?
Has anyone done that for you, lately
or ever? Come over, torn open the sky
and let the snow fall in the wrong month
to show there's a rip in the face of the world?

When the veil lifted

between the worlds, I stood there.
My head had a face.

The first one I saw was my niece.
Now a woman. I knew her from the beauty
mark on her left knee.
Her mother would fall on the ground
all over again like she did at the grave
but she isn't here. My niece walked through.

Then about one million people came by
and I nodded like a crossing guard
of souls with no stop sign or safety vest.
Invisible truly. But I wanted to do my job well.
I wanted to bring my people their people.

My friend's father, who poisoned himself
when she was two, is a force inside her
she tries to wrestle into form. She wants
to make a thing of suffering.

Bastard, I wanted to say when I saw him.
But he was too tragic. Killed by the euphoria
drug his ancestors distilled. Opposites are the same.
Give me a tincture of hell that I might not suffer it.

Then my old neighbour
waved from the balcony in his singlet,
exactly as I remember him. *Come back!* I said.

I saw the grandfather I never wanted to see again.
You don't have a choice when the veil comes down.

I cannot summon my friend's sister, or my lost accountant,
I can't call their names and have it matter.
The drowned, the ones abused by others' fits of power,
or who "fought a courageous battle..." or never said goodbye.

I left my face at the border.
I left my face in case someone should want to cross,
so they should not have to be alone.

Ghosts

Summer morning and the street is half-attended
by ghosts unaware they are visible.
A woman-sized woman in a white T-shirt
echoes my shape. Her gritty voice
comes toward me, swearing
a blast furnace into the sunrise. Moving
as on a hunt, she passes like a death rattle
in my right ear. A man on my left has a pulse
I can't make out till he's beside me and see
he's wearing a mask over his mouth and nose
but also, his eyes. Like a large black bandage,
it swallows his whole face. That square
of paper or cloth is both mystery and urgency,
his upper body tilted toward the dark future
like a ship or a sail. In the next block
a woman on the stoop reports, *I must shower*
and dress every morning. I must.
I have the same urgency
to draw a hard line under my existence,
some guarantee of safety or control,
but it never works. The coffee I order
tastes like earth. No one asked for this.
I walk back among the ghosts,
looking hard at the early world
before the day gets too definite.

All Day I Look at Things

On Thursday at X o'clock, the nice doctor
will give her the shot and she'll go. I plan to be
there with her children, the new elders.
All day I walk around in thirty-degree heat, my toe rubbing
the inside of my leather shoe, reddening. Soon it will bleed.
If I were dying Thursday, this might be
the last smoke bush I see. Its red hair on fire.
And buying ginger ale at the corner store, I stare
at the purple ten-dollar bill a long time, Viola Desmond's face.
Maybe the last purple ten-dollar bill. My last
tea at Annapurna. I don't tell the friendly server
I won't be back.
Somewhere, the waves of the sea are biblical.
Somewhere a ship is capsizing. Somewhere
there is a hurricane, a fire, a herd of elephants,
a boy on a pink tricycle, a garden with a long table
set for dinner with tea lights. Bye world. Bye.

The Night the Rhinos Come

The night the rhinos come we have nowhere else to look.
They are not accusatory, but trot towards us like big dogs.
One turns her face left to show us her profile,
bats one eye at ours and flutters there. To watch
a three-thousand-pound animal flutter is a great gape of awe.

The children shriek: *He's looking at me!*
For size is often male,
and scares or flatters us with its attention.
But she has nothing to do with that.
And trots away.

If this were a dance, we might bow and leave her.
But someone among us is dreaming
power, will buy a rifle,
run out and begin the killing,
is already having nightmares, planning
their illustrious future.

It's still possible to love
how small we are
in the face of her face.

Blue Grit

I feel a derelict sadness. A howling
that began before I had a voice. My howl
is young. Dirty and longing.
Close to a whine, a wail, a horse, a hearse.
It is no singular death but each one
and the man on the corner without teeth
requesting blueberries. Yes, I got them for him
because I was howling though he couldn't see.
I look well but loss knows loss when it sees it.
He told me I was an angel. I felt
like a piece of ephemera. Endless
and open, a plastic bag in the wind.
To give to him was to give to the me beyond me.
Releasing the something I sometimes think I am.
The way the grieving artist said of his painting
that buzzed with a dense concentration of blue grit
at the centre, opening to white at the borders:
The light releases it.

The Party

People are having a party. It's impossible to tell
whether they're in the garden behind me
or in front of me or beside me. The way sound travels
everywhere and in the darkness. But laughter,
these frequent blasts, get louder then quiet
then loud again. Even shrill.
They're hysterically happy, like this is the last time.

~

If the laughing stops in the dark and no one is there to hear it
does it make a sound? Does it make a space
in the dark and become loud in its absence?

~

In spring, four young women sit in front of a house, singing.
They sit on folding chairs, one with a guitar, and sing.
I stop my walking, cry for a minute then listen.
They ask if I want to make a request.

~

I need to write closer to the truth, not the wished-for truth.
To be roughed up a bit. Stop protecting myself from the end.
It's an end not an ending.

~

Four women were sitting singing in the street. Loud.
Last night there was a party. Loud. Then it was over.

~

Yesterday I packed a bag with cans of tuna and beans and corn
and took it to the park where a group of men
who live in the ravine sit in the daytime. I do this when I'm sad
to get out of myself and because they need food.
I leave it by a tree. I don't go too close.

The first time someone chased me.
Is that stuff free? I turned, *Yes, it's for you.*
He thanked me. Today no one noticed by the tree.

I took it closer to the bench, told the man in the red and blue
jersey there's food in it. *OK,* he said. *I'll let them know.*
It was so ordinary I was relieved.
I didn't have to be special, have a good ending.

~

The party next door ended and no one told me.
I just heard it gone. Death is also no one tells you,
and then you're gone.

The party in my body will end. (But the after
might have a sound.)
I'd like to be there when the party stops.

Don't Be Superficial, 'Cause We'll Soon Find Out

At one time, there was the death of a father.
At one time, the death of a brother,
and at one point a brain surgery,
and it was all just one moment.

I'm not just feeling, I'm *seeing.*
And I'm here, committed to breathing,
joy, and painting, until there's nothing left.

I believe in peace with yourself.
And I need to hear my voice. I hear feelings
that are the truth of another.

I don't protest, I profess love
and the abundance of tomorrow
that I may never see.

Vulnerable to

Ancestry

I, descendant of those chased from villages and violated
into violence, inherited the fog of their hiddenness
with more than a wick of dynamite.

Imagine a rider on his fat horse, crop flying.
His dreams and his nightmares made me,
striped me and burned me.

Charred like a train in silence, like a truck of the dead,
like a cold bulb, a dog on the end of a chain
with my food thrown too far.

Laugh, I jump. Stop jumping
and cower. Hung dog in hooded eyes with a fire behind
and the flint in my mouth.

Sadness

Like a nickel lodged in the throat,
shiny but scratched. The taste metallic
with its beaver and edges.

Replace the nickel with a gold coin,
the sadness is only heavier.

Still no one wants it.

If thousands of nickels and
gold coins fall tonight,
the ground will be rich with sadness.

The mouth of the earth is open.

Afterward

Death leaves you so alone.
Your hand goes through a mime's window.
Hello? Anybody there?

Boat

The boat in the water is made of air.

The boat in the air is made of water.

The water is made of ocean and hurry-up.

The ground it's moving away from

is made of goodbye.

Don't Close the Door to the Door to the Door: *happy person with nothing*

Sisyphus Goes Skiing

I'm writing to you from the top of the mountain. Dear friends,
let me tell you, I never expected life to take such a turn.
Icarus just brought me molten chocolate in a paper cup,
and we sit before a fire with our feet up!

This house is of a kind I've never seen before, built of stones
I didn't carry. But someone did, someone got here before me,
before us, and left this place. What did they destroy for our
pleasure? What did it cost them? I don't want to think of it.

It's teeming with the young in brilliant-coloured stretchy outfits
and the strangest boots! Big boots the gods from my
childhood might have worn,
but made of unreal fibres and heavy, so heavy.

But the thing is I got here, and I was carrying nothing!
Just two sticks to help me walk on these long pieces
of wood. I sat in a chair that lifted me high into the trees,
so high I could see the stars in their branches.

And I made it! Am resting. Ic and I so close
to the sun. And I never want to go back down.

For I will consider the awareness

after Christopher Smart

For I will consider the energy breaking into me.

For it is a thief but what it takes costs less than what it offers.

For it is forked and forking and I am its receptor.

For it is shocking as an electric socket and has been in the walls all this time.

For it is indivisible but seems to divide me into Luisa Casati's face in that photo by Man Ray where her eyes are vibrating.

For it makes my eyes vibrate, and the rest of me.

For firstly, it comes to me in the night and is not tender.

For secondly, it pokes me nightly saying, *You awake? You awake?*

For thirdly, in the night it holds court, speaking its languages into my vibrato, my fascia, my organs, my aura.

For fourthly it plays my organs with an inexhaustible source of tunes.

For fifthly, when I'm exhausted, it is never tired. For awareness is never tired.

For sixthly, its company is eternal.

For seventhly, it has not learned to make me a sandwich,
but tells me when it's time.

For it is free.

For it is never not there.

For it is astonishing, untarnished, and shining.

For it cannot be touched.

For it is radiating.

May I?

May first, stick my head out the window
and my face explodes in fireworks.
I have so many eyes. And trumpets!

But there's a hole of pain rushing up to the surface
and through a choke, the words get out,
I'm hardly breathing.

A person is shouting this as crowds of people
die for a million reasons. Can you sweep your hand
across a beautifully-set table and hear the smash?

Ecstasy is not about happiness.
Today I am inside the mouth of the world
where it's hot and wet, stinky like a gourd, and keening.

Today I walked under a tree whose branch
twisted into a symbol I recognized but can't place.
Someone said, it's the editor's mark for *prune me.*

Prune me, said the tree, *cut my branches*
so I can be fatter. It was such a narrow lane.
Where would it grow?

When the plot of land into which I was planted
became too small, I saw I could not grow up indefinitely.
The sky's the limb. Break out.

Before We Were People

I never saw eyes like yours
until the door opened
and there was your father.
Same eyes, wide, brown
and way too beautiful for our species.
You said you often looked away
from others, not to be gazed at.
I would touch your eyeballs
with the tip of my tongue
but there's *you* behind them.
And if you heard me say this,
you'd open them wider
and continue to stare out
with that kind of grace you have,
more llama than human.
Or elk, you'd say.
And me, a bird on your antlers.

Envoy

You are making your way and taking your time about it,
stopping like Orlando in other centuries and bodies,
in zones of affliction and affection.

I thought I was waiting for a lover
but you could be a lesson or a letter
or an orphaned joy carried on the wind.

I'll know you when you get here—but if you don't arrive
I'm waving anyway, because you might need it
on your long road through, the one everyone is taking.

Vows

I courted emptiness for ten years
and it suddenly married me.
Now I'm scared.
But there's no going back.
The cliff has turfed me off
and the birds are flying through me
in their beautiful green and blue birdsmaids' dresses
singing our song. I rejoice with them
until I hear about the thousands of other birds
who've been smashing into windows
and dropping dead, which only makes me
all the more certain of my vows.

Bukowski

One night this guy says I'm not mean enough
or funny enough to be a good poet. He's just read
Bukowski out loud. Bukowski can fight and confide
so why bother? I agree, but say nothing,
which makes me no poet at all now, but a chronicler
who wants to sleep and is awoken by the wish
to be mean and funnier. To be somebody. Like Bukowski.

But when I look, there's a lot of flotsam, some pain
and wishes. My own shenanigans. But nobody here.
Nobody to be. The relief of that is like being let out of a jail
made of my own emojis and desperation.
Or taking my bra off at night.

The difference between a bad poet and a good one is luck,
Bukowski wrote. And having your finger in a light socket.
Bukowski knew he was nobody. That's what makes him so great.
Come to think of it, Emily Dickinson knew first and said so.
Everybody knows they're nobody.
Why is this such a problem for us?

Clothes

I took off my body like a shirt,
and what came out was also me, but empty,

for skin and clothes are just illusion keepers,
and maintenance is a lot of work.

So for a minute, I took off my corset-self
and went flagrant.

If you look with all your eyes
you can see through to the garden behind me.

It helps, I find, to dress for God who, if present
is what everyone wears underneath.

Leap

The raccoon in the tree outside is so
shockingly close to this second-

floor kitchen, its mouth on its brother's neck,
that I want to stop being a person for a while,

full of preference and language.
Existence never stops

being bold. I mean,
aren't they just also looking back?

Cicadas

The cicadas opened a place in the sky and I fell through.
It was dark. All I could see was sound. And mosquitoes.
The great porch music festival of the night.
I fell into it. It's where I wanted to be.
A definite place with a name. Roblin Lake, Ameliasburgh.
But it wasandwasn't the place.

It was the space the place made and the falling
into sound. Warm and still. Voices too,
but cicadas are the dominant species tonight.
And the willow, that in the dark by the lake,
looks like a creature from the deep. I defer to them.
I am so small here. And there are so many I haven't met.

Being Being

Out the window, sun. A kaleidoscope the size of my thumb,
between my thumb and first finger, and the blue sky,
wood trim painted white, round in the lens and twirling
like sun but not sun. Blue itself. The window in view. Seeing.
Seeing while sitting. And watching for nothing but spreading
wider. Seeing that way, this way, is necessary.
Breaks my heart a little. For the enormity
of what comes in through the eyes even when blinking!
Being is being. With assistance. Not a list. A vastness,
without which none of this. Shifting shifts the whole thing
at once. There is no little cataclysm. No little shock.
Little breeze, you art. Little glimpse. Trees, sun.
Nothing is guaranteed, but provisional.
The clock fell off the wall.
The hooks carrying the coats fell off the wall.
The wall let go.

In the Lineage of Asshole Teachers

Milarepa sent his student to the woods
to build him a house. Twelve years. Near starvation.
Gurdjieff said: sell whatever you prize the most.
I thought these were just asshole fables.
Until my teacher sat before me,
his teeth yellow, his eyes blue in their colour,
and mocked every treasured story I offered.
Then he lifted up the broken mirror,
pointed at the fragments
reflecting a warped and partial world,
and told of the whole.
It flashed so quickly into view
I was filled with grief, and nauseating
waves of gratitude.

The High Lonesome

So we were talking in bed, remembering
the junk stores and candy stores, sweet
tarts and licorice pipes. You could already smell
the Dubble Bubble, your hat was in your hands
heading for the door, while I had only one pant leg on.

The building on Yonge Street with cornices like DQ cones
stood lonely and buttressed. When we breathed,
it seemed to whimper. Holly Golightly
later that night sang the high lonesome
in a high-necked gown, quipping and drinking.

We titched the port, ate slices of the Milky Way
cut on the bias, broken
Life Savers, and I put my head
in your lap, and felt that.

Vulnerable to

Grief, Sex, Food

This morning I woke up, still going
after so many seasons.
Best episode ever!
Don't cancel me.
And don't cancel yourself!

Great greedy mouthfuls of longing
and soup.

I saw a couple in a cafe once
and thought I knew them. But didn't.
I heard them speaking
on the grief sex food channel
and thought, *There's only one conversation*
and we're all having it.

This is it! Break my heart again!
Step me back further so I can see wider.
Don't close the door to the door to the door.

Spirit

Descendant of sky water,
plumb line into the nowhere visible below,

but felt through its verging.
Old drone of history, plunge in with your song sword.
I flinch till flensed in sound, no,
in sun darts thrown from elsewhere, coming through
the eyes mouth and heart.

Tonight, you are a cow,

a Jersey cow standing in a valley
in the Alps, a few more cows in the distance.
It's a brilliant sunny day and you can
smell the grass and the cornflowers.

You are not worried about anything.
The farmer is far and the flies lazy.
You hear a horn blow across the field
and moo.

You could've been a moth in a sleeve,
a spider in a sink, a hawk.
You could've been Rembrandt's dog.
Or a fish swimming in cloudy water
and calling it home. But tonight, you are
a cow, what you chose to be.

March 11, 2020

Under My Name

My joy can be a pain to others.
I put words on things no one asked for.
Things shrug them off.

Bird, for instance, is a naked thing,
wing to wing
with a heart in its beating span.

Is there a word that comes before naked?
That's where I want to meet my true pen.

Love Is Not a Pie

I go to bed with Hafiz.
He's the most compassionate person I know.
When friends say they love him too, I'm not jealous.
Love is not a pie, my husband's mother said. Now she's
someone else's mother-in-law, which makes me happy.

Once I thought all answers lay above the neck.
I dreamt Foucault wanted to have sex with me. He said
no one understood him the way I did.
I've never read Foucault. The dream said, *Your lineage is desire,*
sorcery, buffoonery, and everything you have and haven't read.

I'm driving home from the border, past the memory
of last year's retreat, that cacophony and stillness.
Wave to the ghost of my teacher who offered refuge
and took my vows. A ridge of mountains rises
unexpectedly from the plain: quick, *there!*

I write these things down to love them
thinking love is in the pen. But it's here,
in the observable mountains,
and doesn't require writing. It comes up
from the ground, constantly kissing the clouds.

Quick—suffer!

A woman stood in an auditorium and commanded,
Quick–suffer! And we gasped as we knew
it was an impossible instruction. For most suffering
comes in slow, is nursed a lifetime in private
internal revolutions, a drum beat, a hell realm,
a starvation, a memory.

So her instruction, or admonition,
was also permission to release it now,
let it boil and go. As though we could
will suffering to leave us. She simply named
that it is here now and always, as the Buddha said,
not the aberration, but the norm.

And that to know it in ourselves, and then our neighbours,
might release a private suffering
into a kind of public dance, a keening.
She just said it to release the shock so we could begin.

Happiness

Happiness was coming for me   unexpectedly
from the sky

somewhere over Thunder Bay, 1125 miles from where I was
heading, 10:00 a.m. on the wing.

It came rushing in with parcels of air
laden like a Christmas shopper.

No, it was very light.

My eyes had become overstimulated by the brightness
at the window

but couldn't stop looking   we were there   in the air

and the sky was coming for us with everything it carried.

Minutes before it was carrying the worry of the many,

their furrowed foreheads, a knot of worry
promising not to let go.

Then it did—it *did* let go, and outside

it was so sunny it hurt.

And happiness (the only word)

came rushing up like a big bully and pushed right in.

It sounds like bragging, but I could see from this window
that I'm not special.

Happiness was just out there   in the air

and Lord knows what's coming next.

A Full Glass

A few days short of New Year's Eve, a man stands
on the sidewalk, bundled against the dry cold.
He holds a martini glass full of brownish liquid you hope
is hot cider made from September's Macintosh apples
with a bit of ginger or lemon for brightness, though the drink
looks a lot like the slush you're walking on.
To the future! he says to you as you pass.
To the future! you say, holding nothing.

Notes and Acknowledgements

Thank you, awareness / presence / love.

Infinite gratitude to my teachers Ruth Gilbert and Jon Parmenter. "In the Lineage of Asshole Teachers" is for you.

To Alayna Munce for helping me see the book's structure, and its cover, and to Sue Sinclair, my editor and co-conspirator, thank you for your brilliance and for sticking with me. Grateful too for the fresh eyes and tech hands of Manahil Bandukwala.

Thank you to my friends for your support, presence, understanding, and love. I hold you always in my heart.

Much appreciation goes to the Al Purdy A-Frame Association and its members for supporting my residency at the A-Frame where I completed this book.

My sincere thanks go to the people associated with the publications in which some of these poems appeared: *Arc Poetry Magazine, Best Canadian Poetry 2021, Canthius, The Fiddlehead, Grain, The Great Lakes Review, Halibut, Ice Floe Press, Juniper, Literary Review of Canada, The Litter I See, Long*

Con Magazine, The Malahat Review, The Maynard, Periodicities, Queen's Quarterly, the *Tuesday poem* series, *The Walrus, Watch Your Head, Who is your mercy contact?* (Espresso Chapbooks, 2022), and *A Possible Trust: The Poetry of Ronna Bloom*, selected and with an Introduction by Phil Hall (Wilfrid Laurier Press, 2023).

Vulnerable to
The section *Wonder* is for Anita Bloom.

Things He Said the Last Time We Visited is for Andrew Crabtree.

The Buddha Prepares for a Triple Bypass is for Stan Dragland.

Prayer
The Small Nouns Crying Faith is the title of a book by Phil Hall (Book*hug Press, 2013). It is from George Oppen's poem "Psalm."

Speaking Vapour
"Poetry is a hospital for the sane" is from Robert Kroetsch in conversation with Phil Hall.

The Future
The last line of this poem was inspired by the Tom Waits line, "Misery's the river of the soul, everybody row."

Five Elegies
The first elegy is for Martha Baillie and in memory of Christina Baillie. The second elegy is for Jason Mclean. The third and fifth elegies are for Ron Poizner, who I miss a lot. The fourth elegy is for the young girl, Estike, in the film *Sátántangó* by Béla Tarr.

All Day I Look at Things is for Robbie Chesick, Leslie Chesick and Alan Chesick.

Blue Grit is after the painting of the same name by Tim Deverell.

Don't Be Superficial 'Cause We'll Soon Find Out was written for David George Thomas Shipley in the Spontaneous Poetry Booth at Brave: A Festival of Risk and Failure at Harbourfront, Toronto, 2018 and used with permission. That same day, David went to a coffee shop and asked a stranger to read it to him (my handwriting was bad). The stranger, Happie Micha Edwards, went further and made a video featuring both of them, which I discovered by accident. Watch the video of the poem or read the backstory dated November 12, 2018 at ronnabloom.com.

Vows is after Jim Harrison's *Dead Man's Float* (Copper Canyon Press, 2016).

Ronna Bloom is a Toronto-based poet and educator and the author of seven books of poetry. Her work has been broadcast on CBC, recorded by the Canadian National Institute for the Blind, translated into Bangla and Chinese, and appeared three times in *Best Canadian Poetry*. Ronna is also someone who puts poetry to work in the world; she has led initiatives to bring poetry into health care settings, specifically developing the first Poet-in-Residence program at Mount Sinai Hospital/ Sinai Health. Ronna's most recent book is *A Possible Trust: The Poetry of Ronna Bloom*, selected with an introduction by Phil Hall (Wilfrid Laurier University Press, September 2023). www.ronnabloom.com